CONTENTS

KW-054-761

ACKNOWLEDGEMENTS

I am glad to acknowledge the assistance and technical expertise of my colleagues in the Statistics Department of the NFER, particularly Cres Fernandes, the Project Statistician. I am grateful also to Barbara Bloomfield and her colleagues in the Field Research Services Unit for carrying out the administration of the Comparative Reading Survey so efficiently.

I want to express my appreciation to Ann Symmonds, Effie de Souza and Bernadette Hall for word-processing this report, to Mary Hargreaves for preparing the document for publication and to Tim Wright for designing the cover. Enver Carim, NFER's publications manager, oversaw production of this book and we should like to thank him for expediting the process

Alison Tate, my colleague in the Centre for Research in Language and Communication, was responsible for the organisation of the marking of the completed tests and I am very grateful to her for her assistance. I am grateful also to my colleague Anne Kispal, the person mainly responsible for the development of the *Reading Ability Series*, for guiding us in interpreting the patterns of response to the test. NFER-Nelson Publishing Company kindly gave us permission to use the illustration on page 4.

I would like to thank Chris Whetton, the Head of Research Operations at the Foundation, for his helpful suggestions about the research design of the survey; and Derek Foxman, my Head of Department, for his benign oversight and his assistance in editing the report.

Finally, my gratitude is due to the Director of the NFER, Dr. Clare Burstall, for her support and guidance from the initiation of the project to its end.

Tom Gorman

READING IN RECESSION

Tom Gorman
Cres Fernandes

A report on the *Comparative Reading Survey* from
the Centre for Research in Language and Communication,
National Foundation for Educational Research

Published in 1992
by the National Foundation for Educational Research,
The Mere, Upton Park, Slough, Berkshire SL1 2DQ

ISBN 0 7005 1308 6

CHAPTER 1

AIMS AND BACKGROUND

1.1 Introduction

This report presents the results of a survey of the reading performance of two samples of seven- to eight-year-old pupils in Year 3 that was carried out in the spring of 1991. The results were compared with those of a representative sample of pupils who had taken the same test in 1987. The study is therefore referred to as the Comparative Reading Survey.

The report also contains a brief review of some of the factors that might have contributed to the results obtained. The conclusion to the report outlines some of the implications of the study for future research.

1.2 The purposes of the survey

The main purpose of the survey was to provide reliable evidence about the existence and direction of any change in reading standards between 1987 and 1991. This was achieved by comparing the performance of a nationally representative sample of pupils who took a standardised test of reading in 1991 with that of a similar sample of pupils in 1987.[1] In addition, an independent sample of schools that had participated in the original standardisation study in 1987 was invited to retake the test. Again, the purpose was to compare results obtained in 1987 with those obtained in 1991.

A secondary purpose was to relate the test results in both samples to information provided by headteachers in 1991 about approaches to the teaching of reading and writing in the schools involved.

It is stressed that the study was not designed to investigate the effects of particular approaches to the teaching of reading. Nor was the inquiry designed to provide an explanation for any change that might be found, although possible factors relating to such change are briefly reviewed.

---

1   A representative sample of schools is one in which all schools have an equal chance of inclusion. This involves random selection from a data base which includes all schools. A standardised test is one that provides 'standard' scores based on results obtained from a representative sample, adjusted to take account of the ages of the children involved. In this case the scores of pupils who took the test in 1987 were adjusted to have a mean of 100 and a standard deviation of 15.

1.3 The background to the inquiry

In 1990 a group of educational psychologists reported anonymously that reading standards had declined in eight of the local education authorities (LEAs) in which they worked in the 1980s, and in particular in the period since 1985.

In autumn 1990, a team of researchers at the National Foundation for Educational Research (NFER) reviewed evidence made available by LEAs about the reading performance of seven-year-old pupils in the last decade (Cato and Whetton, 1991). The inquiry was commissioned by the School Examinations and Assessment Council (SEAC).

The findings showed that just over half (59 per cent) of the LEAs in England and Wales tested reading performance using objective norm-referenced reading tests. Twenty-six LEAs provided evidence from which trends in performance over time could reasonably be assessed. Evidence of some decline in reading performance was found in 19 of the 26 LEAs.

Indications of change

The trend that was reflected in the results provided by the LEAs emerged most clearly after 1985 and particularly in 1988-90. It was difficult to quantify the magnitude of the decline since the LEAs used different measures and criteria, but the NFER researchers estimated that there was an average decline of one point of standardised score in the mid-1980s and that there had been a further average fall of about one point of standardised score between 1988-90. In the majority of cases where a decline was apparent, this seemed to relate to an increase in the percentage of pupils in the lowest- scoring groups rather than an all-round decline.

While these findings were indicative of a possible change in standards of reading, the research team stressed that it was not legitimate to generalise from this group of LEAs (22 per cent of the total) to the situation in England and Wales as a whole.

The partial nature of the evidence

Statements about changes in standards in the country as a whole need to be based on evidence obtained from nationally representative samples of pupils, and such evidence is only as accurate as the instruments used to detect and monitor such changes.

The NFER review of evidence indicated that the tests used by LEAs to monitor reading were 'generally outdated'. With one exception, the tests had been standardised between 11 and 35 years ago. Some were technically deficient and, in general, the content of the tests did not 'match modern conceptions of reading'. In most cases, the tests were judged to be inadequate in that they did not assess how competent readers actually read in real life: that is, 'silently, through (usually) lengthy passages seeking the meaning of the piece as a whole...'(Cato and Whetton, op.cit.). These factors, the report concluded, 'could to some extent account for a decline in performance' (ibid., p.70).

To obtain reliable results about changes in reading performance over a period of time in England and Wales - and not simply in specific LEAs - it would be necessary to use a test that had been standardised within the last seven years on a nationally representative group of pupils. The procedure used to administer and to mark the test would need to be carefully controlled. As was suggested above, the test would also need to be one which reflected modern conceptions of reading. As these are embodied in the National Curriculum in English, for pupils at Key Stage 2 and above, this would entail, at a minimum, the reading of both fiction and non-fiction with sustained concentration.

1.4 The assessment of reading in the early years

The methods and instruments used in previous national surveys of reading standards and the varying definitions of literacy that have been employed have been reviewed elsewhere (Gorman *et al.*, 1982). Prior to the administration of the Standard Assessment Tasks in 1991, however, there were no government-sponsored national surveys of the reading performance of children in the early years. The best evidence about the literacy attainments of pupils in the past can therefore be derived from research programmes that have been carried out to standardise language tests on national populations. Two such standardisations have been carried out at the NFER since 1986. The results of one of these provided a baseline for the present study.

It is not always realised that any test of reading embodies a particular definition or view of the reading process. Tests that require pupils to read aloud lists of words, such as the Schonell Graded Reading Vocabulary test, imply that reading essentially involves decoding print into sound, a process that some have unsympathetically characterised as 'barking at print'. They test for accuracy of pronunciation rather than for understanding. Tests that involve completing gaps in lists of incomplete sentences, on the other hand, imply that reading primarily involves making sense of the grammar of individual sentences. The two reading tests used in national surveys prior to 1979 were of this nature. It is, however, now generally accepted that fluent reading involves making sense of coherent and complete texts, and that this in turn involves understanding the purpose of a piece of writing and the intentions of the person who wrote it.

The Reading Ability Series

The test used in the Comparative Reading Survey - the *Reading Ability Series, Test A* - meets these specifications (Kispal, Gorman and Whetton, 1989).

The series was developed in 1986, for use with pupils aged 7-13. It comprises a set of six reading tests and an associated Test of Initial Literacy.[2] The tests are arranged in six levels, A - F, each designed for a particular school year-group. The reading tests at each level involve the use of coherent and complete narrative and expository texts.

Rather than presenting the pupil with sentence-completion tasks, lists of words to read aloud or comprehension questions on short extracts, taken out of context - exercises typically found in traditional tests - the test requires purposeful reading of materials similar to those that a pupil would be likely to encounter in and outside the classroom.

In the test taken by children in this study, each pupil had a reading booklet and an answer booklet. The reading booklet was designed and illustrated to look like the type of book the pupil might encounter elsewhere. The answer booklet for this test consisted of open-ended questions requiring the reading and interpretation of three texts. It also required the addition of appropriate words in context.

The first text was a short notice announcing the loss of two kittens. The second was a menu. These two constituted the 'expository' texts and tested the pupils' ability to make use of unambiguous informational material presented in a layout that would aid interpretation. The third text was a short story about a small girl who accidentally pushed a bead into her nostril. It recounts, humorously, the steps taken to have it removed. The story was used as the basis to assess pupils' reading of narrative.

The questions on the expository texts involved the handling of information that a genuine user of such texts would need (e.g. they related to the number of kittens lost, the colour of their fur, and the person to be contacted if they were found; and questions that required the pupils to use the menu to order a meal). The questions accompanying the narrative were ones which an experienced teacher might ask, focusing on the ability to follow the main events in the plot, to appreciate the actions and motives of the characters and to understand the meaning and implications of words and phrases essential to the interpretation of those components of the story. The questions tested the full ability range of the age-group.

---

2   The Test of Initial Literacy provides diagnostic evidence about the reading skills of pupils who are not able to read stories and documentary materials independently. This component of the test was not used in the Comparative Reading Survey, as the intention was to compare the performance of groups of pupils over time, not to diagnose the reading behaviour of individual pupils.

CHAPTER 2

THE SURVEY

2.1 The samples

The Reading Ability Series Test A was completed by two independent samples of Year 3 pupils aged seven to eight in the spring of 1991.

The first sample was made up of pupils from a randomly-selected, nationally representative group of schools in England, selected with reference to region and school type. The achieved sample was made up of pupils in 37 schools (a 52 per cent response rate).

The second was a sample of schools in England and Wales that had taken part in the initial national standardisation exercise in 1987. Twenty-four schools participated (a 69 per cent response rate).

The inclusion of two, independent, samples of schools ensured that the results obtained from one sample would serve either to corroborate or to contradict the results from the other.[3] In all, 2170 pupils participated in the study in 61 schools.

2.2 The test results in brief

In both samples, the fall in average standard scores between 1987 and 1991 was statistically significant. In the nationally representative sample of schools, the average score for pupils in 1987 was 100. In 1991, it was 97.5.

This was fully consistent with the pattern of performance of pupils in the sample of schools that had taken part in the original survey. In 1987, the average score in that sample was 101.3. In 1991, it was 98.7.

---

3   The response rates in the two samples (52 per cent and 69 per cent of schools) were rather low, as indeed were the total numbers of schools involved, 37 and 24. There are, however, other factors relating to the sample which allow credence to be attached to these results. The first is that the results from both samples are in the same direction and of comparable magnitude. The second is that the second sample relates to the same schools: clearly, in these schools, there has been, on average, a decline in performance. The third reason has to do with the nature of non-response in general: if non-respondents were not typical of the population as a whole, they might be expected, on average, to be poorer performers than the national sample. Non-response could, therefore, disguise a larger drop in performance than was found.

The drop in scores was seen both in the test results overall and on all but two of the 25 individual questions. In both years, the narrative section of the test proved to be harder for pupils than the expository one. It was longer and it required an 'appreciation' of the characters and the interpretation of a chain of connected events that made up the plot.

In 1991, pupils found the narrative section even more difficult relative to the expository section than was the case in 1987. On four questions the percentage of pupils answering correctly fell by between four and seven percentage points. This could possibly indicate that pupils in general were less able or willing to engage themselves in this longer text to extract the information they needed. It would, however, be unwise to draw conclusions from this study alone about the fluctuations in relative ease or difficulty of different types of text. But this is an issue on which further investigation would be illuminating.

Figure 1 shows the pattern of results in the sample of schools that was also involved in the original survey. Clearly there has been an improvement in the performance of pupils in some schools, and in one there was a marked rise of over 12 standardised points. In all, nine of the 24 schools (37 per cent) saw an increase in their scores. The magnitude of the rise in these schools is slightly less than the overall fall in the remaining 15 (3.9 and 4.8 standardised points respectively).

As the number of schools in question is very small, it is impossible to draw reliable conclusions about any common characteristics that may be shared by pupils in the schools that showed rising or declining standards. However, none of the nine schools which saw a rise in reading performance was an inner-city school or in an area generally associated with need or social disadvantage. On the contrary, all nine were located in shire counties, rural areas or in middle-class suburbs of larger conurbations. Of the 15 schools where scores fell, seven were in large centres of population or in an industrial region of the country. It is also interesting to note that, in a sample which contained a total of nine church schools, six of these showed an improvement in reading performance between 1987 and 1991.

The picture, then, is one of overall decline in reading standards between 1987 and 1991, with an indication that lower standards may not be general throughout the system.

Figure 1

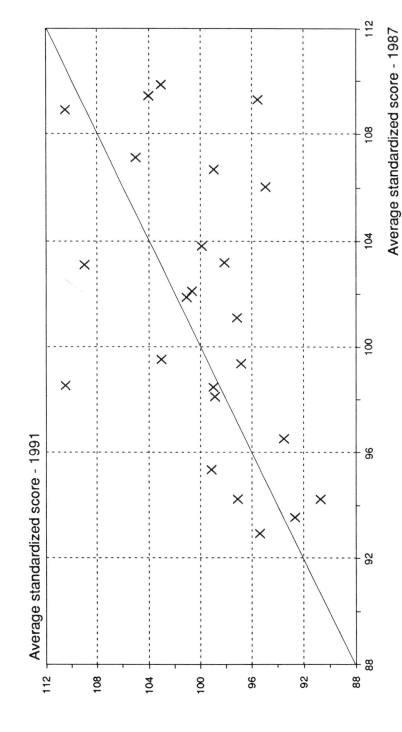

Reading Ability Series Comparability Study
Comparison of average standard scores 1987 and 1991 by school

2.3 The questionnaire to headteachers

Approaches to the teaching of reading

The headteachers in the schools concerned were asked to indicate what approaches were used in their schools to teach reading. The majority of schools (71 per cent) used an approach that involved a combination of reading schemes and 'real books'. Only two schools (four per cent) made exclusive use of an approach involving the use of 'real books'. Fourteen (25 per cent) based their approach on the use of one or more reading schemes.

All but one of the heads (97 per cent) indicated that their staff employed a 'phonic' method of teaching reading. The great majority (84 per cent) also used a 'look-and-say' method.

There is no contradiction inherent in these responses. Pupils are, for example, generally taught to 'sight-read' words of high frequency, particularly where there is an irregular correspondence between the way the word is spelt and the way it is pronounced; and they are also taught to 'sound-out' new words in which this correspondence is more direct. In the one case, a 'look-and-say' method would be applied and, in the other, pupils would need to make use of a knowledge of phonic cues. The different methods are also used by many teachers at different stages of a child's reading development: for example, an initial use of 'look-and-say' techniques will be followed by instruction in 'phonics' as required.

The general pattern of responses was similar to that made by the heads of schools and class teachers in the concurrent NFER Survey of the Teaching of Initial Literacy (Cato *et al.*, 1992). The findings also confirm those reflected in the Annual Report of HM Senior Chief Inspector of Schools for 1989-90, in which he stated that 'there is no evidence of a Gadarene rush into "real books" teaching methods, nor indeed into an exclusive use of any one method' (DES, 1991).

Helping pupils to develop as readers or writers

Heads were asked what additional measures or resources would be helpful in assisting pupils in their schools who had difficulties in reading or writing. Their answers suggested that the greatest need was for more staff time to be devoted to the teaching of reading. Forty per cent indicated a need for additional part-time help for the classroom teacher, and a further 20 per cent referred to the need for additional staff and for time to be focused on 'remedial activity'.

The heads were asked to say whether there were any particular features about the teaching of reading or writing in their own schools that had helped pupils to develop as readers or writers.

A quarter of the heads (26 per cent) acknowledged the value of parental involvement in the teaching of reading. Nine (17 per cent) referred to the good effect of having a school language policy that gave emphasis to the improvement of reading. Others (13 per cent) drew attention to the value of resources such as school and class libraries.

Headteachers' views on reading standards

Heads were also asked whether they had noticed any change in the reading attainments of pupils in this age-group over the past three to five years. Just over half of those responding (57 per cent) said they had. Of these, nine (27 per cent) had detected a 'downwards' trend and ten (30 per cent) a change for the better.

They were then asked to comment on factors that may have contributed to a change in standards of reading. The most common explanation given for a possible decline in standards referred to the effect of recent changes in the curriculum which had meant that time and resources had to be allocated to matters unrelated to the teaching of reading (27 per cent). Other negative factors mentioned were the effect of exposure to television (14 per cent) and changes in teaching methods (14 per cent).

Some heads referred to factors that had positively affected reading performance. These included pupils' exposure to a wider variety of books (16 per cent), and improvement in the quality of resources (14 per cent).

The survey coincided with the first administration in school of Standard Assessment Tasks and Teacher Assessments associated with the National Curriculum. This fact clearly affected the heads' responses to questions related, however indirectly, to the workload of teachers.

Over 80 per cent of those who had discerned a downward trend in reading attainment were also aware of a similar trend in other subject areas, for example, in mathematics.

2.4 Reading methods and reading performance

The information given by heads about the methods of teaching reading in their schools was related to their pupils' test results. A distinction was made between schools in which one or more reading schemes were used, schools which made use of 'real books' only and schools in which a combination of methods was used.

No significant associations were found in this instance between the methods used and pupils' reading performance. However, given the fact that only two schools used a 'real books' approach exclusively, it is not possible to make a statistically valid comparison between these schools and the others in the sample.

The Comparative Reading Survey was not designed to investigate the effects of different methods of teaching reading. A study which did so would need to involve a two-stage survey: firstly, to identify schools using different approaches, by means of questionnaire and case-study techniques; and, secondly, to draw appropriate sub-samples of such schools. More background information, including information about children's knowledge about language and aspects of reading or writing on entering school, would also need to be gathered.

CHAPTER 3

READING ATTAINMENT: THE SCHOOL AND HOME CONTEXTS

In this chapter, some of the factors that have been said to be associated with a change in standards of reading among pupils in the early years will be specified and commented on. Reference is also made to variables that have been shown to be associated with reading attainment in previous studies. Some of these are related to the school environment; others are related to the home.

3.1 The teaching methods used in schools

In recent discussions about the reading standards of pupils in infant and junior schools where a decline has been observed or assumed, a number of commentators have attributed it to the effect of particular methods of teaching reading. Some have ascribed the change specifically to the adoption of what has become known as a 'real books' approach to teaching reading (cf. Turner, 1990). However, after reviewing evidence presented by Mr Turner and his associates, the Education, Science and Arts Committee of the House of Commons concluded that there was 'no reason to believe that, if there has been any general decline in standards, "real books" methods alone have caused it' (House of Commons, 1991).[4]

The most authoritative evidence about teaching methods currently in use in schools is to be found in the HMI report issued in 1991 on the *The Teaching and Learning of Reading in Primary Schools* (DES, 1990).The report reiterated that: 'There was no evidence to show that a single method was overwhelming the teaching of reading.' The great majority of teachers observed, almost 85 per cent, used a blend of methods to teach initial reading skills. More than 95 per cent of the classes used graded reading schemes supplemented by a range of fiction

---

4   There is sometimes a lack of clarity in such discussions which stems, in part, from a misunderstanding of the terms used to describe different methods and materials employed in teaching reading. It is common, for example, to refer to approaches involving 'phonics', 'look-and-say' and 'real books' as if these were three incompatible teaching strategies. 'Real books' actually describes the types of materials used in teaching and indicates that children receive reading instruction using existing works of literature, fiction or non-fiction, rather than through the use of 'reading schemes' which are constructed solely for the purpose of reading instruction. In either case, whether using 'real' books or reading schemes, it is possible to use approaches involving 'phonics', 'look-and-say' and a variety of other strategies, including a 'language experience' approach in which reading material is constructed by the teacher, based on short narratives or accounts given by the child.

---

and non-fiction texts. HMI concluded that in about 20 per cent of the schools, 'the work in reading was judged to be poor and required urgent attention'. 'But', they added, 'serious as that level of poor teaching and learning is, the broad picture has changed little since the findings of the 1978 HMI National Primary Survey' (DES, 1978).

The evidence from both the NFER Comparative Reading Survey reported earlier, and the NFER Survey of the Teaching of Initial Literacy carried out in 1990-91, supports the HMI findings mentioned above and also supports their finding that no more than five per cent of teachers use an approach involving 'real books' exclusively (ibid., 1992).[5]

To say that there has been no radical change in teaching methods in the last decade is not to discount the fact that the 'real books' or 'apprenticeship' approach to teaching reading has influenced teaching and that, in some instances, the principles underlying the approach - all of which are open to question and misinterpretation - have been misapplied (cf. Gorman, 1989). On a separate issue, there is also no doubt that the current dearth of reading schemes with a systematic phonics component has made it difficult for teachers to provide structured instruction in phonics for those pupils who require it (Morris, 1989).

However, research by the NFER indicates that most experienced teachers make use of a range of approaches when teaching the skills involved in word recognition, while at the same time acquainting their pupils with a variety of interesting and attractive books, even before they are able to read these independently (Cato *et al.*, 1992).

3.2 Other possible school factors

At the time that the Comparative Reading Survey was undertaken, schools were in the process of implementing the assessment procedures associated with the National Curriculum at Key Stage 1. The evidence from an evaluation study on the implementation of those procedures suggests that the majority of the teachers involved found the workload that was entailed in keeping records and in conducting Teacher Assessments and Standard Assessment Tasks to be

---

5   In April 1990, members of the Centre for Research in Language and Communication at the NFER began a survey of the teaching of initial literacy in Year 2 classes (the SOIL Survey). The survey included a questionnaire study of a random sample of 122 schools and a case study of 26 schools. The questionnaire study was undertaken in autumn 1990 and the visits to schools between January and June 1991. Concurrently, a survey of the teaching of initial literacy was undertaken in a random sample of 30 schools in one local education authority, and visits were made to ten schools in that authority.

'heavy' or 'very heavy' (SEAC, 1992). Teachers had also been involved in some of the initial processes of implementing the National Curriculum in the previous year (1989-90) when the pupils in this study had been in Year 2. It is not clear, however, to what extent this could have influenced their reading standards in 1991. In any case the influence of the implementation of the National Curriculum would not account for a change in standards of reading in the mid-'eighties; nor is such an effect likely to occur to the same degree in subsequent years, as various measures have been taken to lessen the impact of the National Curriculum assessment procedures on classroom practice. It is, therefore, clearly necessary to consider other factors that might have caused or contributed to a decline in standards. Some of these relate to home circumstances.

3.3 Home factors in reading performance

Numerous research studies have provided information about ways in which a child's home life influences his or her reading attainment. One source of evidence of particular interest is that given in the second report of the National Child Development Study (NCDS)[6] which dealt with seven-year-old children born in 1958. Evidence was associated with a number of background variables, including aspects of the family situation, such as whether or not the child was living with both natural parents; the degree of parental interest in the child's educational progress; and patterns of employment within the family.

Each of these sets of factors was shown to affect children's attainment in reading. The NCDS study indicated that reading attainment was significantly lower for those whose family situation was 'atypical': this was equally true for boys and girls.[7]

More recent studies have confirmed that children's literacy and numeracy skills on entry to school are related to several aspects of their home background. The homes of successful readers typically provide a variety of contexts for making use of reading and writing. In such homes, literacy is integrated into different aspects of family life. Moreover, there is research evidence to show that there is a strong relationship between children's knowledge of literacy at age five and their subsequent achievement.

---

6   The National Child Development Study is a longitudinal study involving children born in a particular week in 1958. A preliminary report on the study, based on a sample of over 10,000 children, was included in the second volume of the report of the Central Advisory Council for Education in England on Children and their Primary Schools (DES, 1967).

7   The researchers examined the performance of children living with both their own natural parents and of children in what was termed 'atypical' family situations, i.e. children who were reported as having one natural parent because of illegitimacy, desertion, divorce, separation or death; those with one step-parent; and those who were adopted, fostered or in care.

Research by Tizard and Hughes (1984) in nursery schools highlighted the contrasts in the patterns of language use between children at home in conversation with their mothers and children at school in conversation with teachers. The research indicated that 'the home provided a more fertile environment for language learning than the school'.

The same patterns of use and interaction were observed by Wells and his colleagues in their longitudinal study of 138 children in Bristol. Wells concluded: 'As with other researchers who have compared the language experiences of younger children at home and in the nursery or pre-school playgroup, what we have found is that, compared with homes, schools are not providing an environment that fosters language development' (Wells, 1987).

Given this evidence about the effects of aspects of family life on children's attainments in language and literacy, it is necessary to consider which factors might have particular relevance to the reading attainment of the pupils in the 1991 sample. Three associated sets of variables which have affected the home life and pre-school environment of the children in the 1980s appear to be relevant. These are:

(i)   **Changing patterns of family life and composition, most notably the marked rise in the proportions of single-parent families or households headed by a lone parent, usually the mother.**

Evidence of financial disadvantage in such families is to be found in the results of the 1989 General Household Survey. This indicated that over half (52 per cent) of one-parent families lived in households with a weekly income of £100 or less compared with only five per cent of married or cohabiting families. In contrast, 46 per cent of married or co-habiting families lived in households with a weekly income of more than £350, with only eight per cent of one-parent families living in such circumstances (OPCS, 1991).

(ii)   **Changes in patterns of employment, most notably the rise in absolute levels of unemployment among men and the increase in the proportion of married women, with children under five, who have paid employment.**

In relation to the latter, in 1985, 27 per cent of women with children aged under five went to work (seven per cent full time and 20 per cent part-time). In 1990, on the other hand, 41 per cent of women with dependent children under five were in paid employment (12 per cent full-time and 29 per cent part-time).

(iii)   **The corresponding growth in the number of establishments providing substitute-care for children under five.**

Just as different home environments may produce different effects on language and cognitive development, 'differences in day care environments may have similar effects' (Melhuish *et al.*, 1990). There is research available to show that 'the quality of the day care environment appears to have a profound effect upon language development' (McCartney, 1984).

There has been a great increase in the last decade in the proportion of children under five who receive day care. The largest increase proportionally has been in care provided for children aged two to four. Over 80 per cent of children aged three to four attended some form of care in 1990. (These figures exclude day-care by relatives, particularly grandmothers, who continue to provide the most common form of non-parental care used by working parents.)

According to Moss (1991), there are aspects of day care that mark Britain out from most other countries. These are: the low level of public sector involvement; the concentration on part-time places; the poor pay and conditions of most of the workers; and large variations in provision between local authorities.

Facilities for day care provision in schools were also expanded in the 1980s. LEAs have increasingly allowed children to enter school from the age of four years, where, in reception classes, they are generally judged to be given too formal a teaching programme (Sylva, 1991).

CHAPTER 4
SUMMARY AND CONCLUSIONS

In the Comparative Reading Survey, a recently standardised test was used to investigate the comparative performances of nationally representative samples of Year 3 children in 1987 and 1991. The test was more in tune with modern conceptions of reading than those in use in a number of LEAs, some of which had shown a decline in reading performance since the mid-'eighties.

Two samples of pupils were used in the Comparative Reading Survey in 1991: one consisted of 24 schools which had participated in 1987, and the other was an independently drawn nationally representative sample. The results supported the conclusion that there had been a decline in overall performance over the period of the two test administrations. Although response rates were low, there was convincing evidence of the generalisability of findings, firstly, because of the decline in the performance of the sample of schools that participated on both occasions, and, secondly, because the extent of the overall fall in performance in that sample was similar to the fall in performance in the independent, national sample of schools.

There was some indication that the decline in performance in response to the more difficult questions in the test, those relating to the narrative texts, was greater than that on questions relating to expository texts. Because of the size of the sample involved, it is not possible to present this as a reliable finding, but one which serves as a hypothesis that warrants further investigation.

While the results of the Comparative Reading Survey show an overall fall in performance from 1987 to 1991, there was some indication in the data that this decline may not have been general throughout the educational system. This conclusion is derived from the results of the sample of 24 schools that participated on both occasions. Nine of the schools had an improved performance in 1991 as compared with 1987.

Other data on reading performance suggest that a decline began in the mid-'eighties, and this raises a question about whether there were changes in the extent of disadvantage to children during the period. It is the case that, during the 1980s, the number of one-parent families increased considerably and, with this circumstance, the need for the parent - nearly always the mother - to go out to work. In turn, this has created an increase in the requirements for day care facilities and increased the pressure on schools to accept four-year-olds, when the education they provide is not always appropriate for such young children.

17

When the downward trends were first revealed in the monitoring data of a number of LEAs, they were blamed on changes in methods of teaching reading. It was said that the growth of the use of 'real books' was the cause. Subsequent research by the NFER and observation in schools by HMI have established that there has been no such radical change in the methods of teaching reading and that experienced teachers use a judicious mix of methods. These include phonics, 'look-and-say', and, on appropriate occasions, they use 'real books' as a resource and not as a method of teaching. About five per cent of schools appear to have changed to an exclusive 'real books' approach. Any effect of this on standards of overall performance, up or down, would be small.

Other factors which have been mentioned by teachers as possibly associated with reading performance include the teachers' industrial dispute in the mid-'eighties and, more recently, the heavy workload on teachers due to the implementation of the National Curriculum.

Whether any one of the suggested home or school factors is most responsible for the significant changes in performance found in the Comparative Reading Study, or whether they have a joint effect, it is clear that some of the factors specified could equally affect other subject areas. It is known that, in some contexts, the scores of pupils in mathematics as well as reading have declined in recent years. For example, research conducted by the NFER in Croydon, prior to the Survey of the Teaching of Initial Literacy, showed that performance in mathematics had shown the same pattern of decline as performance in reading in the period 1988/87 to 1989/90 (London Borough of Croydon, 1992).

Overall the results of this study suggest research questions in five areas:

(i)   What aspects of reading are most affected by any changes in performance?

(ii)   What pre-school factors are associated with reading performance?

(iii)   What school factors are associated with reading performance?

(iv)   What changing home circumstances are likely to affect reading performance?

(v)   Is performance in other subjects equally affected by home or school factors?

We conclude that there is an urgent need for a research study that would investigate the differential effect of home, pre-school and school factors in relation to children's literacy and other basic skills in the early years.

REFERENCES

CATO, V., GORMAN, T.P. , KISPAL, A. and FERNANDES, C. (1992). *How Do Teachers Do It? The Teaching of Reading and Writing to 7-Year-Olds*. Slough: NFER.

CATO, V. and WHETTON, C. (1991). *An Enquiry into Local Education Authority Evidence on Standards of Reading of Seven-year-old Children*. A report by the National Foundation for Educational Research. London: Department of Education and Science.

DAVIE, R., BUTLER, N. and GOLDSTEIN, H. (1967). *From Birth to Seven. The second report of the National Child Development Study*, in association with the National Children's Bureau. London: Longman.

DEPARTMENT OF EDUCATION AND SCIENCE (1978). *Primary Education in England*. London: HMSO.

DEPARTMENT OF EDUCATION AND SCIENCE (1990). *The Teaching and Learning of Reading in Primary Schools*. A Report by HMI. London: HMSO.

DEPARTMENT OF EDUCATION AND SCIENCE (1991). *Standards in Education 1989-90*. The Annual Report of HM Senior Chief Inspector of Schools. London: HMSO.

GORMAN, T.P., WHITE, J., ORCHARD, L. and TATE, A. (1982). *Language Performance in Schools. Primary Survey Report No.2*. London: HMSO.

GORMAN, T.P. (1989). *What Teachers in Training Read about Reading*. Centre for Research in Language and Communication. Occasional Paper 4. Slough: NFER.

HOUSE OF COMMONS EDUCATION, SCIENCE AND ARTS COMMITTEE (1991). *Standards of Reading in Primary Schools*. Third Report of 1990/91 Session. Vol.1.

KISPAL, A., GORMAN T. P., and WHETTON C. (1989) *Reading Ability Series Levels A-F, Teacher's Handbook*. Windsor: NFER-NELSON.

LONDON BOROUGH OF CROYDON (1992). *Reading Competence at Age 7*. London: London Borough of Croydon Education Department.

McCARTNEY, K. (1984). 'Effects of quality of day-care environment on children's language development', *Development Psychology*, 20, 244-60.

MELHUISH, E.C. (1990). 'Research on day care for young children in the United Kingdom.' In: MELHUISH, E.C. and MOSS, P. (Eds) *Day Care for Young Children, International Perspectives*. London: Routledge.

MELHUISH, E.C., LLOYD, E., MARTIN S. and MOONEY, A. (1990). 'Type of day care at 18 months - II. Relations with cognitive and language development', *Journal of Child Psychology and Psychiatry,* 31, 860-70.

MORRIS, J.M. (1989). 'Linguistics in a lifetime of learning about language and literacy.' In: HUNTER-CARSCH, M. *The Art of Reading.* Oxford: Blackwell.

MOSS, P. (1991). 'Day care policy and provision in Britain'. In: MOSS, P. and MELHUISH, E. (Eds) *Current Issues in Day Care for Young Children: Research and Policy Implications,* 22-101. London:HMSO.

OFFICE OF POPULATION CENSUS AND SURVEYS (1991). *General Household Survey,* Preliminary Results for 1990. London: OPCS Monitor SS91/1.

SCHOOL EXAMINATIONS AND ASSESSMENT COUNCIL. (1992). *An Evaluation of the 1991 National Curriculum Assessment, Report 3: Further Evidence on the SAT: Manageability and Relationships with Teacher Assessment.* Slough: NFER/BGC Consortium.

SYLVA, K. (1991). 'Educational aspects of day care in England and Wales.' In: MOSS, P. and MELHUISH, E. (Eds) *Current Issues in Day Care for Young Children: Research and Policy Implications,* 118-30. London: HMSO.

TIZARD, B. and HUGHES, M. (1984). *Young Children Learning, Talking and Thinking, at Home and at School.* London: Fontana.

TURNER, M. (1990). *Sponsored Reading Failure.* Education Unit, Warlingham Park School.

WELLS, G., BARNES, S. and WELLS, J. (1984). *Linguistic Influences on Education and Attainment. Final Report to the DES of the Home and School Influences on Educational Attainment Project.* Bristol: Centre for the Study of Language and Communication, School of Education, University of Bristol.

WELLS, C.G. (1987). *The Meaning Makers. Children Learning Language and Using Language to Learn.* London: Hodder and Stoughton.